BASIC/NOT BORING
LANGUAGE SKILLS

WORDS & VOCABULARY

Grades 4-5

Inventive Exercises to Sharpen
Skills and Raise Achievement

Series Concept & Development
by Imogene Forte & Marjorie Frank

Exercises by Sheri Preskenis

Illustrations by Kathleen Bullock

Incentive Publications, Inc.
Nashville, Tennessee

About the cover:

Bound resist, or tie dye, is the most ancient known method of fabric surface design. The brilliance of the basic tie dye design on this cover reflects the possibilities that emerge from the mastery of basic skills.

Cover art by Mary Patricia Deprez, dba Tye Dye Mary®
Cover design by Marta Drayton, Joe Shibley, and W. Paul Nance
Edited by Tama Montgomery

ISBN 0-86530-401-7

PRINTED IN THE UNITED STATES OF AMERICA

TABLE OF CONTENTS

CELEBRATE BASIC LANGUAGE SKILLS

Basic does not mean boring! There certainly is nothing dull about . . .

> . . . deciding if you would *jeer* at a *stingray* or *bargain* with a *barracuda*
>
> . . . figuring out whether you would find a *subpoena* or a *bathyscaphe* in the ocean
>
> . . . wondering what to do with a flounder
>
> . . . finding words to name the fear of water, germs, cats, or closets
>
> . . . looking for words on the beach after dark or rescuing words from a shipwreck
>
> . . . using synonyms to help a crab complete an obstacle course across a beach
>
> . . . explaining how the treasure chest got to the bottom of the ocean
>
> . . . untangling an octopus and a squid or coming face-to-face with a shark

These are just some of the adventures students will explore as they celebrate basic language skills. The idea of celebrating the basics is just what it sounds like—enjoying and improving the basic skills of reading, understanding, and using words and language. Each page invites learners to try a high-interest, visually appealing exercise that will sharpen one specific language skill. This is not just an ordinary fill-in-the-blanks way to learn! These exercises are fun and surprising. Students will do the useful work of practicing language skills while they enjoy the interesting adventures of characters on the beach and in the ocean. And, at the same time they practice basic word skills, they will be sharpening thinking skills, too.

The pages in this book can be used in many ways:
- for individual students to review or practice a particular skill
- to sharpen the skill with a small or large group
- by students working on their own
- by students working under the direction of an adult

Each page may be used to introduce a new skill, reinforce a skill, or assess a student's ability to perform a skill. And, there's more than just the great student activities. You will also find an appendix filled with resources for students and teachers—including a ready-to-use test for assessing these words and vocabulary skills.

It is intended that an adult be available to assist the students as needed with their learning and practice. Students will need to have a good dictionary available for completing some of the word activities.

As your students take on the challenges of these word adventures, they will grow! And as you watch them check off the basic language skills they've strengthened, you can celebrate with them!

The Skills Test

Use the skills test beginning on page 56 as a pretest and/or a post-test. This will help you check the students' mastery of basic word and vocabulary skills and will prepare them for success on achievement tests.

SKILLS CHECKLIST FOR
WORDS & VOCABULARY, Grades 4-5

✔	SKILL	PAGE(S)
	Learn and use new words	10–17
	Learn new words in a variety of categories	10–17
	Use a dictionary to find word meanings	10–18, 38, 39, 44, 45
	Use context clues to determine a word's meaning	18, 19
	Choose the correct word for a particular context	19, 32–34, 38, 39
	Identify words used correctly in context	19, 38, 39
	Identify the meanings of common prefixes	20, 21
	Recognize and use prefixes to determine meanings of words	20, 21
	Identify the meanings of common suffixes	22, 23
	Recognize and use suffixes to determine meanings of words	22, 23
	Identify the meanings of common root words	24, 25
	Recognize and use roots to determine meanings of words	24, 25
	Recognize and use synonyms	26–29
	Recognize and use antonyms	30, 31
	Identify and use homophones	32–34
	Distinguish between homophones; select correct one for a context	32–34
	Distinguish between words that have similar sounds or spellings	32–34, 38, 39
	Distinguish between words that are easily confused with one another	32–34, 38, 39
	Recognize, form, and use compound words	35
	Identify and define multiple meanings of a word	36, 37
	Identify and use figurative language	40–42
	Classify words according to meaning and use	43
	Distinguish between denotation and connotation	44, 45
	Give the denotation and connotation of words	44, 45
	Explore the history and origin of words	46, 47, 50
	Use a dictionary to find information about word history and origin	46, 47, 50
	Use correct words to complete analogies	48, 49
	Find the origin of words borrowed from foreign languages	50

WORDS & VOCABULARY

Skills Exercises

COULD YOU?...WOULD YOU?...SHOULD YOU?

Could you float on a *catamaran?* Would you swim in a *maelstrom?* Should you dive into a *maw?* You can't answer these questions unless you know what the words mean!

Use your dictionary to find the meanings of the words in bold. Then write your answer to each question. Be ready to explain your answers!

1. Could you float on a **catamaran?** _____

2. Would you swim in a **maelstrom?** _____

3. Should you dive into a **maw?** _____

4. Could you catch a fish in a **coupe?** _____

5. Would you see a **manatee** at a **matinee?** _____

6. Should you bargain with a **barracuda?** _____

7. Could you sniff an **aroma** on the beach? _____

8. Would you give a **marimba** to a **mollusk?** _____

9. Should you **prevaricate** to the lifeguard? _____

10. Could you take a rest in a **bungalow?** _____

11. Would you be **cordial** to a **carnivore?** _____

12. Should you float into a **treacherous** current? _____

13. Could you float on a **foible?** _____

14. Would you enjoy listening to a **monotonous** song? _____

15. Should you **aggravate** an eel? _____

Name

SHOULD YOU?...COULD YOU?...WOULD YOU?

Should you *jeer* at a *stingray?* Could you swim with a *connoisseur?* Would you wear a *garish* bathing suit? You can't answer these questions unless you know what the words mean!

Use your dictionary to find the meanings of the words in bold. Then write your answer to each question. Be ready to explain your answers!

1. Should you **jeer** at a **stingray?** _____

2. Could you swim with a **connoisseur?** _____

3. Would you wear a **garish** bathing suit? _____

4. Should you get **lethargic** in big waves? _____

5. Could a floating raft be **conducive** to sleeping? _____

6. Would you rub **coarse** sand on your body? _____

7. Should you be **punctual** to your lifeguard class? _____

8. Could you **contrive** a way to fix a broken surfboard? _____

9. Would you be **valiant** or **tremulous** if you met a shark? _____

10. Should you **chide** your little sister for swimming alone? _____

11. Could you cause a **calamity** with a beach umbrella? _____

12. Would you throw out **rubbish,** or keep it? _____

13. Should a **novice** play in a championship game of beach volleyball? _____

14. Could you get along with an **obstinate** neighbor? _____

15. Would you feel comfortable around a **famished** shark? _____

Name _____

WHERE WOULD YOU FIND THIS?

Fisherman Fred has found some very strange things in his net. Is that where they belong? Decide where each one of these things would be found. Circle the correct choice. You will need to use your dictionary!

Where would you find . . .

5. . . . **a molar?**
   a. making a movie
   b. in your mouth
   c. riding a motorcycle

1. . . . **a gam?**
   a. at a computer
   b. in the ocean
   c. in a candy store

2. . . . **a chauffeur?**
   a. in a shoebox
   b. in a coffee cake
   c. driving a car

3. . . . **a lexicon?**
   a. floating in a pool
   b. in a library
   c. acting on stage

4. . . . **some borscht?**
   a. in a hardware store
   b. on a menu
   c. talking on the phone

6. . . . **a euphonium?**
   a. in a bucket
   b. growing on a tree
   c. in an orchestra

7. . . . **a vicar?**
   a. on a sundae
   b. in a church
   c. in a toolbox

8. . . . **a sternum?**
   a. in your body
   b. singing in a choir
   c. in a dresser drawer

9. . . . **a mariner?**
   a. sailing a ship
   b. growing in a garden
   c. in a salad

10. . . . **a matinee?**
    a. at a movie theater
    b. at a wedding
    c. snorkeling at a reef

11. . . . **an attorney?**
    a. in your bloodstream
    b. in your bank account
    c. in a courtroom

12. . . . **nuptials?**
    a. in a church
    b. on a sandwich
    c. on the moon

13. . . . **a subpoena?**
    a. in a shell
    b. in an envelope
    c. in a fishing boat

Name

WHERE WOULD YOU FIND THAT?

Fisherwoman Freeda has found some more weird stuff in her net. Decide where each one of these things would be found. Circle the correct choice. You will need to use your dictionary!

Where would you find . . .

1. . . . **some kelp?**
   a. in a fishing net
   b. under a bed
   c. at a wedding

2. . . . **an anemone?**
   a. at the dry cleaners
   b. in a tide pool
   c. under a desk

3. . . . **a procession?**
   a. in a parade
   b. in a science textbook
   c. on a hamburger

4. . . . **an eclipse?**
   a. in a lake
   b. on a quilt
   c. in the sky

5. . . . **a caddie?**
   a. inside a camera
   b. in your blood
   c. on a golf course

6. . . . **a garnish?**
   a. on a dinner plate
   b. in a poem
   c. riding a pony

7. . . . **a sequoia?**
   a. in some soup
   b. in a forest
   c. inside your ear

8. . . . **a patella?**
   a. under your skin
   b. on a fishing hook
   c. in a history book

9. . . . **a martinet?**
   a. in a car engine
   b. in a puppet show
   c. on a banana split

10. . . . **a bathyscaphe?**
    a. in the ocean
    b. inside a glove
    c. at a wedding

11. . . . **a manta?**
    a. on a space ship
    b. in a fishing net
    c. under a bed

12. . . . **a stethoscope?**
    a. under a ski lift
    b. around a doctor's neck
    c. on a snowplow

13. . . . **a villain?**
    a. in a movie
    b. in a flower pot
    c. under a toenail

Name _____

WHAT WOULD YOU DO WITH IT?

Julianne has found an unusual use for a flounder!
What would you do with a flounder?

Look at each of the words below. Circle the
most reasonable thing to do with each of
the items listed. You may need some help
from your dictionary!

What would you do with a . . .

1. **flounder?**   use it as a bookmark   fry it for lunch   wear it on your head

2. **plankton?**   put it on a pizza   feed it to a fish   write a letter on it

3. **snorkel?**   live in it   take it swimming   fry it with bacon

4. **brooch?**   bury it   write to it   put it in a jewelry box

5. **scoundrel?**   tickle it   avoid it   water it

6. **grotto?**   explore it   color it red   make noise with it

7. **query?**   clean it with soap   plant it   find an answer to it

8. **rumba?**   mail it   dance it   dress it up

9. **soufflé?**   measure it   bake it   wear it to dinner

10. **trophy?**   show it off   melt it   sing to it

11. **banister?**   slide on it   plant it   put frosting on it

12. **marimba?**   feed it   dance with it   make music on it

13. **foe?**   wrap it up   draw with it   make friends with it

14. **sophomore?**   send it to school   paint it   put it on a sandwich

15. **sieve?**   slice it   put it in the bank   pour water through it

16. **architect?**   boil it   hire it   put it in an envelope

Name

A CASE OF AQUAPHOBIA

If phobia means "fear," can you guess what *aquaphobia* is? Get a clue from the picture! Use your glossary to track down these *fear* words. Write the letter of the picture or word that matches each fear.

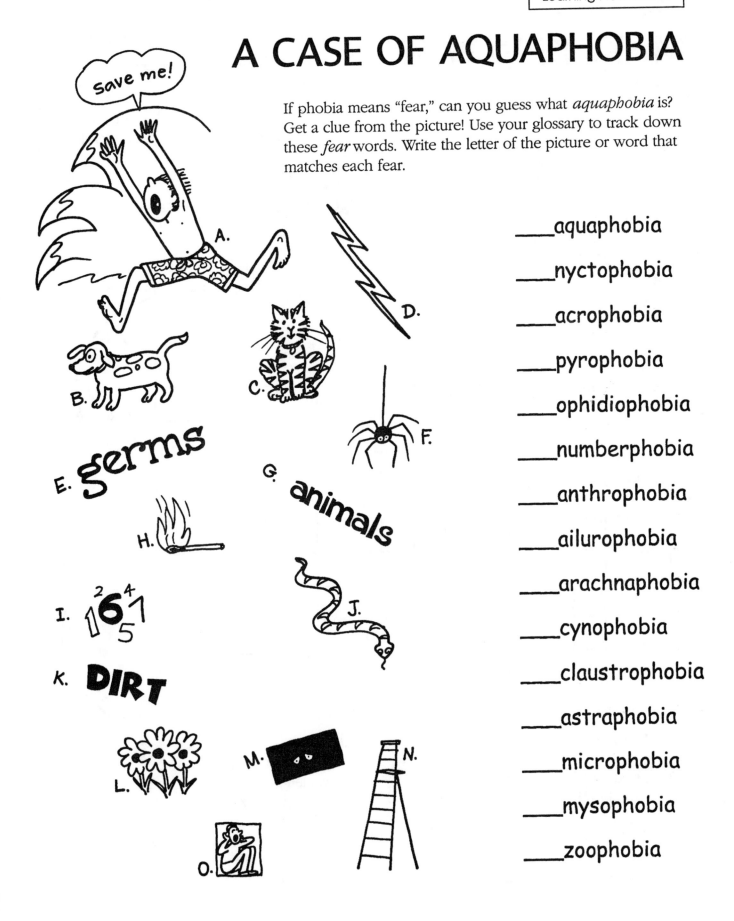

____aquaphobia

____nyctophobia

____acrophobia

____pyrophobia

____ophidiophobia

____numberphobia

____anthrophobia

____ailurophobia

____arachnaphobia

____cynophobia

____claustrophobia

____astraphobia

____microphobia

____mysophobia

____zoophobia

Name _____

MAKING WAVES

It's a huge wave! The biggest waves in
the world are caused by earthquakes.
What is this kind of wave called? Find
its name and the other answers in the
word bank to solve the puzzle.

WORD BANK

fjord	weed
tsunami	sea
ichthyologist	mariner
habitat	archipelago
ecology	trough
grotto	abalone
flotsam	

DOWN

1. a shell lined with mother-of-pearl
2. the study of natural environments
3. natural setting where an animal lives
4. a cave
7. a tidal wave
8. a sailor
10. kelp is a kind of sea_____

ACROSS

5. the lowest point in a wave
6. a scientist who studies fish
9. floating wreckage
11. a group of islands
12. a long, narrow inlet of the sea between tall, rocky cliffs
13. the ocean

Name

AFTER DARK

There's nothing quite like the beach at night! Everything looks, sounds, and feels so much different after the sun goes down and the shadows take over.

Look at the words at the bottom of the page. Find the meaning of each word and write it on the line. Then search the picture for something to match each word. Color that part of the picture with the color written next to the word. (*Ex: Find something to match the word* **vessel**, *and color it blue.*)

vessel	_____ (blue)	merriment	_____ (green)
lunar	_____ (yellow)	pentapod	_____ (pink)
luminous	_____ (orange)	gritty	_____ (beige)
biped	_____ (red)	murky	_____ (gray)
savory	_____ (white)	kindling	_____ (brown)

Name _____

HOT BEACH...COOL DRINKS

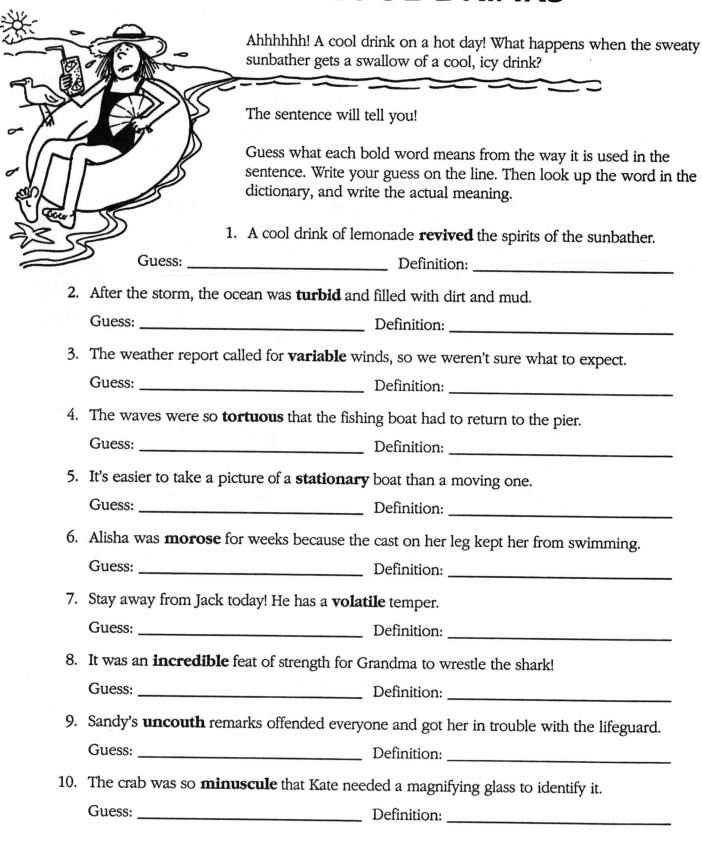

Ahhhhhh! A cool drink on a hot day! What happens when the sweaty sunbather gets a swallow of a cool, icy drink?

The sentence will tell you!

Guess what each bold word means from the way it is used in the sentence. Write your guess on the line. Then look up the word in the dictionary, and write the actual meaning.

1. A cool drink of lemonade **revived** the spirits of the sunbather.

   Guess: _____ Definition: _____

2. After the storm, the ocean was **turbid** and filled with dirt and mud.

   Guess: _____ Definition: _____

3. The weather report called for **variable** winds, so we weren't sure what to expect.

   Guess: _____ Definition: _____

4. The waves were so **tortuous** that the fishing boat had to return to the pier.

   Guess: _____ Definition: _____

5. It's easier to take a picture of a **stationary** boat than a moving one.

   Guess: _____ Definition: _____

6. Alisha was **morose** for weeks because the cast on her leg kept her from swimming.

   Guess: _____ Definition: _____

7. Stay away from Jack today! He has a **volatile** temper.

   Guess: _____ Definition: _____

8. It was an **incredible** feat of strength for Grandma to wrestle the shark!

   Guess: _____ Definition: _____

9. Sandy's **uncouth** remarks offended everyone and got her in trouble with the lifeguard.

   Guess: _____ Definition: _____

10. The crab was so **minuscule** that Kate needed a magnifying glass to identify it.

    Guess: _____ Definition: _____

Name

SUNKEN TREASURE

A treasure chest has been sitting on the bottom of the ocean for years. How did it get there? These words sank along with the treasure, but some words are missing from the tale!

Read the 10 possible explanations, and write in the missing words. Choose a word from the chest that will make each sentence meaningful.

How Did the Treasure Get Here?

1. A crafty pirate pushed it overboard from his ship and _____ to find it later.

2. It was _____ off an island by a _____ tidal wave.

3. Someone found it in a pirate's cave and threw it off a high _____ into the ocean.

4. The chest was picked up by a whirling _____ and dropped into the ocean.

5. It fell overboard from a ship being _____ around in a wild _____ .

6. Two divers _____ the chest off a beach at midnight and _____ it here.

7. It slid into the _____ during a terrible, shaking _____ .

8. A whale's _____ knocked it off the deck of a pirate _____ .

9. A pirate ship _____ against the rocks and _____ in a hurricane.

10. No one really knows how the chest got here!
    It is a huge _____ .

ocean   washed   storm   hid   earthquake   mystery   crashed   huge   tail   shook   bridge   tornado   violent   dragged   sank   ship   tossed   intended

BEACH BEHAVIOR

There's a bit of misbehavior at the beach today! What does *misbehavior* mean? The prefix, *mis*, changes the word *behavior* to a word that means "bad behavior."

A **prefix** changes the meaning of the root word in some way. Look at the meanings of the prefixes on the chart. Use these to write the meaning of each word below.

Meanings of Some Prefixes

a	(on)
anti	(against)
be	(make)
dis, im, un	(not)
inter	(between)
mid	(middle)
mini	(small)
mis	(bad, wrong)
multi	(many)
over	(too much)
pre	(before)
re	(again)
sub	(under, below)
trans	(across)
uni	(one)

Write the meaning of each word with a prefix.

1. unicycle _____

2. ashore _____

3. befriend _____

4. subnormal _____

5. misspell _____

6. overpriced _____

7. midfield _____

8. antiwar _____

9. transatlantic _____

10. afoot _____

11. rewrite _____

12. predawn _____

13. multicolored _____

14. impossible _____

15. minivan _____

16. interstate _____

17. unfriendly _____

18. dishonest _____

Name _____

A BIPED ON A UNICYCLE

This biped on a unicycle is showing off his biceps to the camera on the tripod!

A **prefix** is a word part that can be added to the beginning of a word to change the word's meaning. Some prefixes come from numbers. When they are added to words, they create a word that has a number built into it! Pay close attention to the meanings of these prefixes as you follow the directions below.

Prefix Meanings

uni	(one)	hepta	(seven)
bi	(two)	octo	(eight)
tri	(three)	non	(nine)
quad	(four)	deca	(ten)
penta	(five)	centi	(hundred)
hex	(six)		

1. Draw an octopus riding a unicycle.	3. Draw some binoculars inside a pentagon.	5. Draw a decapod crawling on a hexagon.
2. Draw a tricycle inside a quadrilateral.	4. Draw a centipede sleeping in a heptagon.	6. Draw a triangle inside a nonagon.

Name _____

PERIL AT SEA!

What will happen to the storm-tossed ship? Maybe these words will give you a clue. The meanings of the suffixes will help you explain what these words mean. Write the meaning of each word on the line near the word.

Suffix	Meaning
en	(to make)
ful	(full of, like)
fy	(to cause to be)
ic	(like, pertaining to)
ism	(act or quality of)
less	(without)
lets	(small)
ment	(act or quality of)
ness	(state or condition of)
or	(one who)
ous	(full of, like)
ship	(state or quality of)
some	(full of)
ward	(toward)
y	(like, full of)

A **suffix** is a word part that can be added to the end of a word to change the word's meaning.

EXCITEMENT

PERILOUS

ROCKY

STORMY

FRIGHTEN

NERVOUS

HORRIFIC

SEAWARD

FEARFUL

HARDSHIP

HOPELESS

COURAGEOUS

SURVIVOR

DANGEROUS

TERRIFY

DROPLETS

LOSTNESS

SAILOR

TROUBLESOME

HEROISM

Name

22

SHARK ALERT!

There are more than 250 different kinds of sharks! How many of them have you met?
Find out a fact about two of them. Choose a suffix from the rocks to make a word that matches each meaning. Write the boxed letters in order on the answer lines to discover the names of these two sharks.

This spotted shark can grow to be 6 feet long!

1. full of treachery ☐ __ __ __ __ __ __ __ __

2. someone who dives __ ☐ __ __ __ __

3. relating to magic __ __ ☐ __ __ __ __ __

4. to make deep __ __ __ __ ☐ __

5. to make afraid __ ☐ __ __ __ __ __ __

Answer: A ____ ____ ____ ____ shark.

This shark lives along the shores of warm oceans near the mouths of rivers. Some even live in fresh water.

6. toward the sky __ __ __ ☐ __ __ __

7. full of hunger ☐ __ __ __ __ __

8. pertaining to the ocean __ __ __ ☐ __ __ __

9. able to break __ __ __ __ __ __ ☐ __

10. state of being sharp __ __ __ __ __ __ ☐ __

Answer: A ____ ____ ____ ____ ____ shark.

ward (toward)

ic (pertaining to)

ness (state of being)

en (to make)

er (one who)

ous (full of)

ry (full of)

able (able to be)

al (relating to)

Name _____

23   *Basic Skills/Words & Vocabulary 4-5*

UNFORGETTABLE!

When you come face-to-face with a weird sea creature, it is a truly unforgettable experience! The word *unforgettable* is built from the root word *forget*. Then other word parts (a prefix and a suffix) are added to the word. If you know your roots, you can create and figure out all kinds of words!

Choose the right root from the box to form each of the words described.

Root	Meaning
act	(act, do)
aqua	(water)
carn	(flesh)
dorm	(sleep)
dynam	(energy)
flam	(burn)
fug	(flee)
labor	(work)
mon	(warn)
phobia	(fear)
port	(carry)
scend	(climb)
tele	(far)
vis	(see)

1. _____ivore   eater of flesh

2. zoo _____   fear of animals

3. _____itive   one who flees

4. ad_____ition   warning

5. _____ible   able to be seen

6. _____tic   pertaining to water

7. _____ion   the act of doing

8. _____mable   easily burned

9. de _____   climb down

10. _____tic   full of energy

11. _____itory   place to sleep

12. _____scope   instrument for seeing far

13. trans _____   carry across

14. _____atory   place to work

15. arachna _____   fear of spiders

16. _____able   able to be carried

17. phobo_____   fear of fear

18. a _____   to climb up

uh oh!

Name _____

SUBMARINE WATCH

Root	Meaning
ann	(year)
aqua	(water)
ast	(star)
auto	(self)
bene	(good, well)
bio	(life)
cycl	(circle)
frag	(break)
geo	(earth)
graph	(write)
grav	(heavy)
labor	(work)
lib	(book)
loc	(place)
mar	(sea)
meter	(measure)
mini	(small)
mot, mov	(move)
ped	(foot)
pend	(hang)
port	(carry)
sol	(sun)
vac	(empty)
term	(end)

The submarine travels close to the bottom of the ocean. It's down there moving around among the roots! *Submarine* is a word that is formed from the root word *mar*, meaning "sea," and the prefix *sub* and suffix *ine*. Read the roots and their meanings. Then add suffixes and/or prefixes to the roots to form some words. Try to make at least 20 words!

Name

THE BEACH CONNECTION

What's the connection between all this stuff left lying around on the beach? The connection is **synonyms.** Draw a path to help the crab get through the maze and across the beach to meet his friend. The path can only touch items that contain pairs of synonyms. You might need some help from your dictionary!

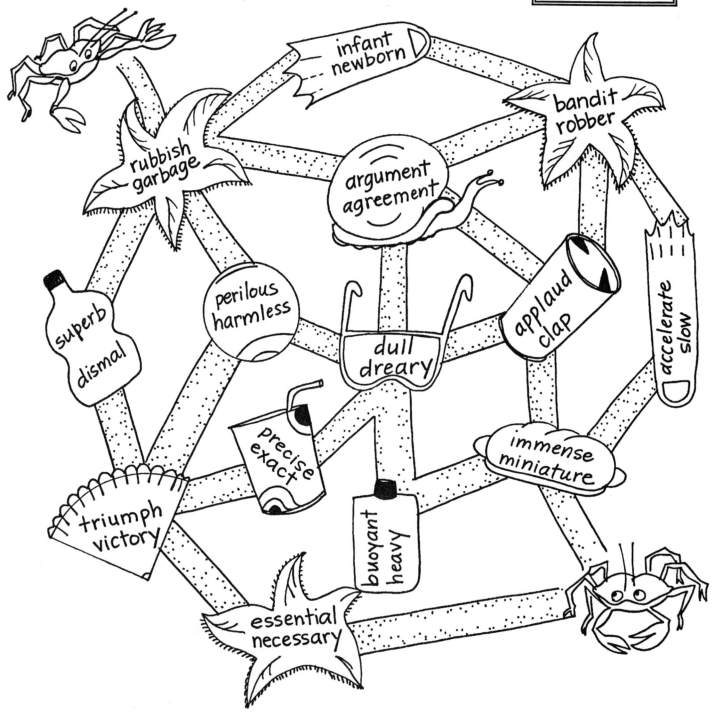

infant
newborn

bandit
robber

rubbish
garbage

argument
agreement

superb
dismal

perilous
harmless

dull
dreary

applaud
clap

accelerate
slow

precise
exact

immense
miniature

triumph
victory

buoyant
heavy

essential
necessary

Name

WILD SURF

Synonyms are words that have the same or similar meanings.

Sal is working at staying on top of the wave. The words in the surf didn't do so well. They've been tossed around and totally scrambled! Each word in the list below has a synonym lost in the waves. First, find the matching wave-tossed synonym for each word. Then unscramble the synonym, and write it on the line.

1. thrilling _____

2. amateur _____

3. feat _____

4. incredible _____

5. danger _____

6. astonish _____

7. massive _____

8. respond _____

9. slobber _____

10. genuine _____

11. gesture _____

12. horde _____

13. horror _____

14. journal _____

15. penalize _____

2. vonice

3. eded

1. tixcenig

4. baiblevunlee

5. ripel

6. zamae

7. eugh

8. warnes

9. lorod

10. laer

11. tovememm

12. omb

13. rerrot

14. raidy

15. shinup

Name _____

27 *Basic Skills/Words & Vocabulary 4-5*

IMPOSTORS IN THE SAND

Figure out which word in each sand castle is the impostor!

Three of the words in each castle are synonyms. Cross out the one that does not mean the same as the others. Do it quickly—before the tide comes in and washes the sand castles away!

> **Synonyms** are words that have the same or similar meanings.

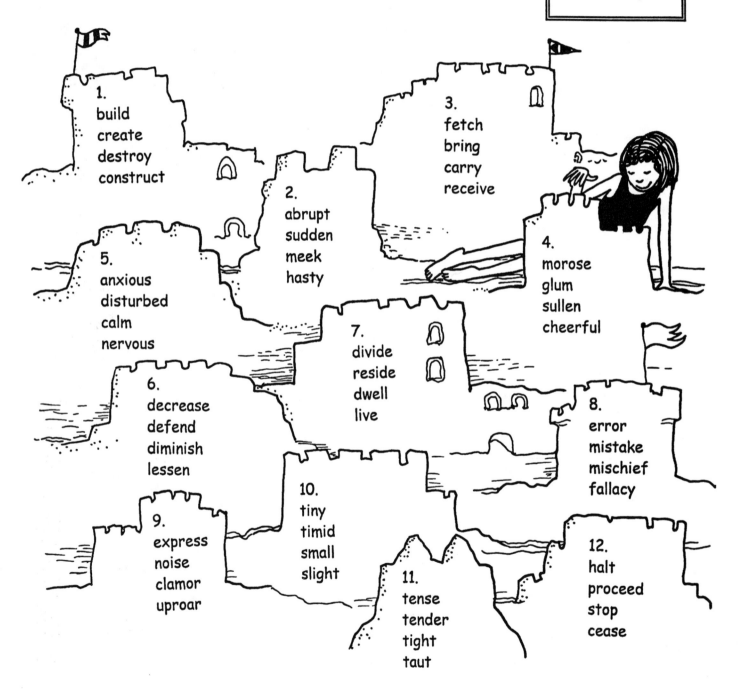

1. build
create
destroy
construct

2. abrupt
sudden
meek
hasty

3. fetch
bring
carry
receive

4. morose
glum
sullen
cheerful

5. anxious
disturbed
calm
nervous

6. decrease
defend
diminish
lessen

7. divide
reside
dwell
live

8. error
mistake
mischief
fallacy

9. express
noise
clamor
uproar

10. tiny
timid
small
slight

11. tense
tender
tight
taut

12. halt
proceed
stop
cease

Name

BEACH BLANKET MATCH-UP

Synonyms are words that have the same or similar meanings.

Every word on George's beach blanket has a matching synonym on Georgia's blanket. Can you find the matching pairs? Use a marker or crayon to circle each word in the pair and draw a line to connect them. Use a different color for each pair of synonyms. Then choose two words, and write them in a sentence.

_____

_____

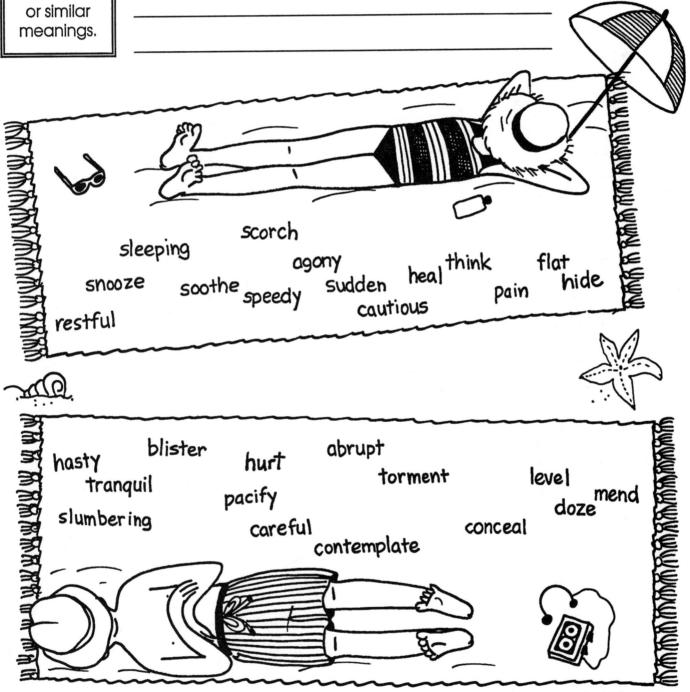

scorch

sleeping

agony   think   flat

snooze   soothe   speedy   sudden   heal   pain   hide

cautious

restful

blister   abrupt

hasty   hurt   torment   level

tranquil   pacify   mend   doze

slumbering   careful   conceal

contemplate

Name _____

29

AU / LCCC
Teacher Educational Resource Center
1005 North Abbe Road
LR 216
Elyria, Ohio 44035

Basic Skills/Words & Vocabulary 4-5

LITTLE SHOP OF OPPOSITES

> **Antonyms** are words that mean the opposite of each other.

When customers come to the beach shop, they seem to say the opposite of what they mean!

Write the antonym for each word in parentheses to make the sentences correct.

1. "This shop has the (worst) stuff on the beach!" _____

2. "Let's get some (bad) quality diving supplies." _____

3. "Everything in this shop is too (cheap) for me to afford." _____

4. "I'll loan you some money," said my (Uncle) Martha. _____

5. "My swim mask and snorkel are always (straight)." _____

6. "I need to (sell) a(n) (ugly) (old) swimsuit." _____

   _____ _____

7. "The wet suit is so (light)—it must weigh a ton!" _____

8. "This is on sale because it has a (temporary) stain." _____

9. "Look at what a (stingy) size this raft is!" _____

10. "These beach towels are made of a really (flimsy) fabric." _____

11. "What an (ordinary) color this shirt is!" _____

12. "Won't you need two (weak) people to carry this boat?" _____

Name _____

DON'T OBEY THE SIGNS!

Antonyms are words that mean the opposite of each other.

Every sign and title on the beach today says the opposite of what it should!

Read each sign, label, and title. Look for one word that could be replaced with its opposite. Cross out that word and write its antonym to change the meaning of the message.

Name

THE WHOLE IN THE PALE

Homophones are words that sound alike but have different spellings and meanings.

What's wrong with this title? It's a case of mixed-up homophones! What should it be?

_____

Read about all the happenings on the beach today. Choose the right homophone for each sentence.

1. Chester decided to _____ (berry, bury) Angelina.

2. Who wants to run _____ (straight, strait) into the ocean?

3. "You _____ (through, threw) that too high!" hollered Josie.

4. "I _____ (caught, cot) it anyway!"

5. Don't you think that the _____ (sees, seize, seas) are pretty wild today?

6. That dead fish is giving off a very _____ (foul, fowl) odor.

7. Don't trip over the _____ (pale, pail)! You'll _____ (brake, break) a leg!

8. Erwin went to the fishing _____ (peer, pier) and caught six fish in one _____ (hour, our).

9. Who _____ (beet, beat) Oliver in the surfing contest?

10. Aunt Fannie _____ (taught, taut) me how to build cool sand castles.

11. Let's _____ (buy, by) _____ (some, sum) cotton candy at the pier.

12. I can't! I only have twenty _____ (cents, sense).

13. The hot sun is burning my _____ (feet, feat).

14. Two squawking seagulls _____ (flu, flew) toward my potato chips!

15. When the hurricane comes, the tourists will _____ (flee, flea) from the beach.

Name _____

A WHALE OR A WAIL?

Homophones are words that sound alike but have different spellings and meanings.

What is the lifeguard hearing from the water: a *whale* or a *wail?*

Which homophone is the right word to answer this question?

_____

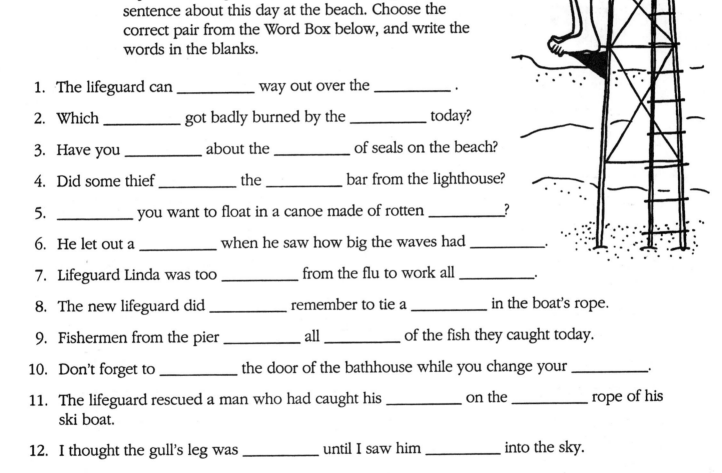

A pair of homophones is needed to complete each sentence about this day at the beach. Choose the correct pair from the Word Box below, and write the words in the blanks.

1. The lifeguard can _____ way out over the _____ .

2. Which _____ got badly burned by the _____ today?

3. Have you _____ about the _____ of seals on the beach?

4. Did some thief _____ the _____ bar from the lighthouse?

5. _____ you want to float in a canoe made of rotten _____?

6. He let out a _____ when he saw how big the waves had _____.

7. Lifeguard Linda was too _____ from the flu to work all _____.

8. The new lifeguard did _____ remember to tie a _____ in the boat's rope.

9. Fishermen from the pier _____ all _____ of the fish they caught today.

10. Don't forget to _____ the door of the bathhouse while you change your _____.

11. The lifeguard rescued a man who had caught his _____ on the _____ rope of his ski boat.

12. I thought the gull's leg was _____ until I saw him _____ into the sky.

Word Box

sea	see	herd	heard	not	knot
grown	groan	steal	steel	eight	ate
son	sun	wood	would	clothes	close
sore	soar	weak	week	toe	tow

Name _____

WHAT YOU SEE IN THE SEA!

What Ramon sees in the sea is a lot of weird fish! Each fish has a pair of homophones. Choose eight pairs, and write a sentence for each that uses both words in the pair. Try to make the sentences tell about something that can be seen in the sea!

> **Homophones** are words that sound alike but have different spellings and meanings.

tail tale

flea flee

wear where

cell sell

toad towed

throne thrown

scene seen

right write

raise rays

dents dense

which witch

Steal steel

plain plane

higher hire

1. _____

_____

2. _____

_____

3. _____

_____

4. _____

_____

5. _____

_____

6. _____

_____

7. _____

_____

8. _____

_____

Name

SHIPWRECK!

Diver Delbert was amazed to find a shipwreck loaded with words! Oddly enough, every one of these words could be part of a compound word, like the word *shipwreck*.

Using the words on the boat as one part of the compound, make as many compound words as you can. You can make a compound word by adding another word to the beginning or the end of one of these words. Use two words from the boat, or add other words not found here! Write the words you create in the middle of the page. If you need more space, use the back of the page.

> A **compound word** is a word made up of two complete words joined together.

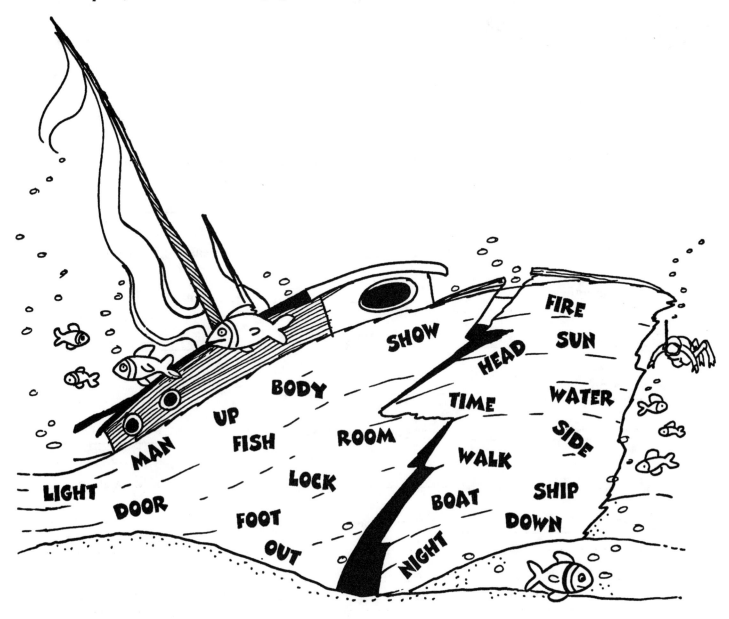

Name

35   *Basic Skills/Words & Vocabulary 4-5*

BEWARE OF CRABBY CRABS!

YOWL!!

Take that!

The same word has two different meanings! There are many other words like *crab*—words that can mean two or more things, even though they look and sound the same! Can you think of some others?

In the examples below, write two different meanings for the word given. If the word is not given, read the meanings and decide what the missing word is!

1. _____ **crab** _____

2. the opposite of up _____ the feathers on a duck

3. an animal footprint _____ a place to run races

4. _____ **date** _____

5. to bounce or jump up _____ the season after winter

6. to remove from a job _____ something that burns

7. _____ **fly** _____

8. a dot on a ladybug _____ to see something

9. _____ **shower** _____

10. a home for a pig _____ an instrument for writing

11. _____ **box** _____

12. a tiny insect that digs into
    the skin and buries its head _____ a sound made by a clock

Name _____

STARS ON THE BEACH

Gloria thought she was the star of the beach! Now she has to share the spotlight with another star. What are these two meanings of the word *star*?

1. _____

2. _____

The other words around this page also have more than one meaning. Choose any three of them.
For each word you choose, illustrate two or more meanings of the word in one of the circles.

Everybody wants to be a star!

Gloria Glamorous

out

set

arms

pupil

trunk

coast

saw

pick

bridge

bat

fence

run

ride

quarter

back

down

time

line

count

light

Name _____

OCTOPUS OR SQUID?

People are always getting an octopus mixed up with a squid! If you want to keep from confusing these two words, you need to know the meaning of each one. There are many words that get confused with others because the two words have similar meanings or looks. Each of these examples has a pair of words that often get confused with each other. Circle the correct word to answer each question.

1. Carlos found a sea creature with ten arms around its mouth.
   Did he find an **octopus** or a **squid?**

   Tangled up again !

2. After dinner, Jana ate her cheesecake on the beach.
   Was this her **desert** or her **dessert?**

3. The large floating object with a bell marks the channel for boats.
   Is this an **anchor** or a **buoy?**

4. Jay and Sheri like to sit on the beach at night and study the stars.
   Are they studying **astrology** or **astronomy?**

5. Jenna is always saying words that are the opposite of what she means!
   Does she speak in **antonyms** or **synonyms?**

6. The beach club throws a huge midnight beach party every two years.
   Is this an **annual** event or a **biennial** event?

7. Kai just bought a new boat and wants to protect it in case of damage.
   Should he buy **assurance** or **insurance?**

8. The weatherman brought an instrument to the beach to measure the wind.
   Did he bring an **anemometer** or a **barometer?**

9. When we were surfing, we saw several pieces of floating wreckage from a ship.
   Did we see **flotsam** or **jetsam?**

10. When kids drove their motorbikes in circles around our blanket, we were upset!
    Did we give a **compliment** or a **complaint** to the lifeguard?

11. We saw a streak of light flash through the sky, then a large rock crashed to the beach.
    Was the thing that landed a **meteor** or a **meteorite?**

Name

HOW MANY WHALES?

Only four of the twenty whales are jumping today. Is this the *majority* or the *minority?*
People often get these two words confused. Do you know what each one means?
There are many words that get confused with others because the two words have similar meanings or looks. Each of these examples has a pair of often-confused words. Circle the correct word to answer each question.

1. Four of the twenty whales are jumping today.
   Is this the **majority** or the **minority?**

2. Natalie's doctor told her that she has strep throat.
   Is this a **diagnosis** or a **prognosis?**

3. We'll cook our clam chowder over low heat for a long time.
   Will we let the soup **simmer** or **boil?**

4. Those flowers by the pier only last for one year, then they need to be replanted.
   Are they **annuals** or **perennials?**

5. Hannah won free surfing lessons for perfect attendance at school this year.
   Were the awards given by the **principle** or the **principal?**

6. Barb's mom just finished writing a children's story about manatees.
   Will she get a **copyright** or a **patent** for her book?

7. Three friends found a redwood tree. They measured it by reaching their arms around the
   trunk and holding each other's hands.
   Did they measure the **circumference** or the **diameter?**

8. A widespread storm with high winds brought huge waves crashing against the island.
   Was this a **tornado** or a **hurricane?**

9. I found some sea glass that light could pass through, but I couldn't see through it.
   Was this glass **transparent** or **translucent?**

10. The sailor offered to take our whole group to the island for free. We said, "Yes!"
    Did we **except** or **accept** his offer?

Name

HAPPY AS A CLAM

Are clams really happy? How do you know? What does it mean when someone is "happy as a clam" or "mad as a wet hen"? These are examples of figurative language. They have a meaning that is a little different from what the words actually say.

At the beach picnic, all these friends and family members are using figurative language. Write what each saying really means! Then, on the back of this page, draw what each saying would look like if the words meant what they actually say!

_____

_____

_____

_____

_____

_____

_____

Name

40

GOOD TASTE IN FRIENDS

What does it mean to have "good taste in friends"? Does it have anything to do with eating your friends? No! It's just an example of figurative language. The meaning is different from what the words actually say.

At the beach picnic, all these friends and family members are using figurative language. Write what each saying really means!

Name _____

HO, HUM!

Samantha's letter to her friend Bo is full of figurative language.

Circle all the examples of figurative language you can find in her letter. Try to find out what each one means, if you don't already know!

How many examples of figurative language did you find?

_____

Dear Bo,

Ho, hum! What a dull, dull day! Here I sit in this new bathing suit that cost me an arm and a leg, with the sun beating on me, the waves pounding like drums, and the seagulls squawking as loud as a choir. I love the beach—just like my dad. I'm a chip off the old block! The water and sky are as pretty as a picture.

I do love the beach, but nothing is happening! Yes, the crabs are racing around faster than greased lightning, but there's no real action! My day is as dry as dust and as dull as a doorknob.

If only something outrageous would happen, this could turn out to be a red-letter day. I wish a giant waterspout would go bananas across the ocean. Or I wish a lifeguard would blow her top and go off her rocker right in front of everyone. Or wouldn't it take the cake if a dreadful sea monster appeared in the water, breaking up ships like toothpicks? Just think of how people would go running down the beach, scared stiff and screaming bloody murder! And wouldn't it be the last straw if all this happened, and I missed it because I was sleeping?

Well some say, "Out of sight, out of mind," but I say that absence makes the heart grow fonder. I miss you. I wish I could just snap my fingers and you'd be here, quick as a wink! Make no bones about it, today is a wipe-out! If only you were here, then this day would not be deader than a doornail!

Love,
Samantha

Help!

Help!

Help!

Name _____

42

THE SHIRT DOESN'T FIT

Which volleyball player's shirt just doesn't fit with the rest? All the words have something in common— except this one:

_____

In each line below, three of the four words have something in common. Decide what these three words have in common. Write the category on the line. Then cross out the word that does not belong in that category.

1. walrus   whale   dolphin   lizard   _____

2. kelp   chowder   flotsam   jetsam   _____

3. bandit   anchor   smokestack   lifeboat   _____

4. snow   sleet   rain   wind   _____

5. lobster   wren   pigeon   heron   _____

6. wail   screech   shriek   mumble   _____

7. monitor   ruler   keyboard   mouse   _____

8. wrench   wok   blender   skillet   _____

9. anemone   scorpion   coral   octopus   _____

10. cactus   bucket   sand   kite   _____

11. receiver   index   binding   title   _____

12. ligaments   liver   spaghetti   muscles   _____

13. salmon   steelhead   redwood   flounder   _____

14. vicar   attorney   priest   preacher   _____

15. stumble   leap   skip   hop   _____

16. cub   duckling   lamb   duck   _____

17. blizzard   hazard   tornado   hurricane   _____

18. frog   snake   turtle   lizard   _____

Name _____

MAROONED!

Looks like trouble, doesn't it! This poor guy is *marooned*. What does that mean?
The **denotation** (dictionary definition) of the word is pretty simple. The **connotation**
(suggested meaning) can be much more complicated and may be more interesting!
Write the denotation and connotation for each word below.

MAROONED

Denotation: *Left alone on a deserted island*

Connotation: *starving, thirsty, in danger, hopeless, sunburned, ragged clothes, no escape, death*

PIRATE

Denotation:_____

_____

Connotation:_____

_____

_____

_____

SUNBURN

Denotation:_____

_____

Connotation:_____

_____

_____

_____

I'm sunburned and marooned on a deserted island. Surrounded by sharks and pirates and there's a storm coming!

SHARK

Denotation:_____

_____

Connotation:_____

_____

_____

_____

STORM

Denotation:_____

_____

Connotation:_____

_____

_____

_____

ISLAND

Denotation:_____

_____

Connotation:_____

_____

_____

_____

Name _____

BON VOYAGE!

"Bon voyage!" is what people say when you leave on a ship. It means "Good trip on the water!" "Trip on the water" is only the **denotation** (dictionary definition) of the word *voyage*. This word might also make you think of wild waves, rough seas, adventure, mystery, fog, whales, sharks, pirates, or big parties. All of these things are the **connotations** (suggested meanings) of the word!

Read each of the definitions below. Write **D** next to each denotation. Write **C** next to each connotation. Then figure out what the word is, and write it in the box!

1.
_____ a large body of salt water

_____ cold, waves, surfing, deep, monsters, fish, swimming, drowning, hurricanes, sailing, diving, fun, danger, beaches

2.
_____ cold, penguins, danger to ships, shipwrecks, tall, mysterious, white

_____ a large, floating mass of ice detached from a glacier

3.
_____ splash, dive, float, wet, cold, wave jumping, beaches, summer, pools, fun, danger

_____ to propel oneself through the water by natural means

4.
_____ a mollusk with eight muscular arms lined with suckers

_____ ugly, creepy, squeezing, big eyes, grabbing, wrapping, danger, scary, hiding beneath the water

5.
_____ a small, strong, buoyant boat carried by a ship

_____ emergency, danger, rescue, oars, stormy seas, sinking ship, sharks, screaming people

6.
_____ fun and excitement, adventure, sunshine, skiing, swimming, relaxing, travel, trip, family, money

_____ time spent away from home for a rest, change, or break from something

7.
_____ something of value accepted as an exchange for buying goods; usually coins and/or paper

_____ wealth, savings, banks, toys, buying, spending

Name _____

WORDS WITH A PAST

Did you know that the word *fudge* was supposedly named after Captain Fudge, a seaman who had a reputation for not telling the truth? Today, when you fudge on the truth, it means that you're not telling the whole story! Many words have interesting histories. A good dictionary will give you the history, or **etymology,** of many words. Often it is in brackets at the end of the definition.

fret (fret) v. 1. to cause to be uneasy; distress, vex 2. to gnaw or wear away
(Middle English freten, to devour or eat away)

Use your dictionary to find out something about the history of some of these words. Learn about at least 10 of them. Find out what or who the word was named after, or discover something about its meaning.

1. Ferris wheel _____
2. Frisbee™ _____
3. March _____
4. Monday _____
5. angel _____
6. guppy _____
7. cologne _____
8. magnolia _____
9. teddy bear _____
10. pedigree _____
11. leotard _____
12. comet _____
13. paper _____
14. sardine _____
15. Chihuahua _____
16. America _____

Name _____

TASTY WORDS

Macaroni Market

Graham Cracker Cafe

Frank's Frankfurters

The Doughnut Hang-Out

the Waffle Place

Banana Splits

Olive's Omelettes

TORTILLA TIME

The Fudge Shop

tangerine smoothies

How in the world did anyone ever think of *waffles*—pancakes with funny little holes in them? Where did the word *omelette* come from, anyway? And how did crackers get named *graham?* Many of the foods we eat have interesting names from unusual places. See if you can find out something about the etymology of these food words.

> An **etymology** is a word history. A good dictionary contains etymologies of many words. These can be found in brackets before or after the definition.

Try to find the etymology for at least 10 of these foods.

1. macaroni _____

2. graham crackers _____

3. frankfurter _____

4. doughnut _____

5. waffle _____

6. banana _____

7. omelette _____

8. tortilla _____

9. tangerine _____

10. mushroom _____

11. cabbage _____

12. chocolate _____

13. spaghetti _____

14. tapioca _____

Name

SWIMMERS' LINE-UP

When the swimmers want to swim, you'll find them in the ocean. When they want to ride a great new roller coaster on the boardwalk, however, they have to wait in a line. There's a special way to show the relationship between words. It's called an **analogy**. It shows that two pairs of words have the same relationship.

> **Example:** swim : ocean *as* wait : line (swim is to ocean *as* wait is to line)
> Swim is something people do in the ocean. Wait is something they do in a line.

Circle the correct word to fit in each blank in these analogies.

1. mask : face *as* flippers : _____
   swim   feet   dive   equipment

2. sunglasses : eyes *as* _____ : skin
   water   nose   sunscreen   sunburn

3. money : _____ *as* lunch : lunchbox
   buy   pocket   change   spend

4. snorkel : _____ *as* raft : float
   mask   swim   bubbles   breathe

Complete these analogies:

5. tired : sleep *as* hungry : _____

6. swim : _____ *as* jog : road

7. library : books *as* _____ : dishes

8. glass : _____ *as* paper : tear

9. _____ : lumber *as* wheat : flour

10. years : age *as* degrees : _____

11. wet : _____ *as* gritty : sand

12. hand : fingers *as* _____ : pages

13. _____ : dog *as* fins : fish

14. row : oar *as* sweep : _____

Name

BOARDWALK ANALOGIES

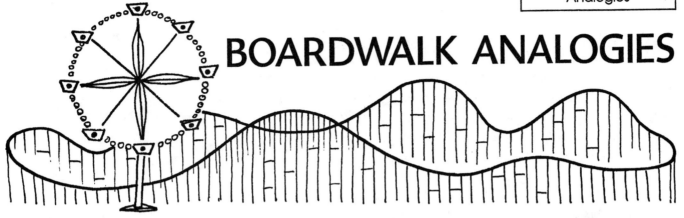

The boardwalk has great rides. The beach has great dunes.
You can use an analogy to compare the two.

Example: rides : boardwalk *as* dunes : beach
(Rides are to the boardwalk *as* dunes are to the beach.)

In an **analogy,** both pairs of words have the same relationship.

Fill in the blanks to complete each analogy.

1. legs : lifeguard *as* _____ : octopus

2. tidepool : anemone *as* _____ : horse

3. _____ : sailing *as* racquet : tennis

4. siren : _____ *as* cotton candy : taste

5. weight lifter : weights *as* _____ : surfboard

6. pelican : pelicans *as* mouse : _____

7. warm : _____ *as* cool : cold

8. playground monitor : playground *as* _____ : beach

9. calm : stormy *as* _____ : exciting

10. sun : light *as* stove : _____

11. _____ : bird *as* skin : person

12. rain : hurricane *as* _____ : blizzard

Can you finish these? There are several right answers.

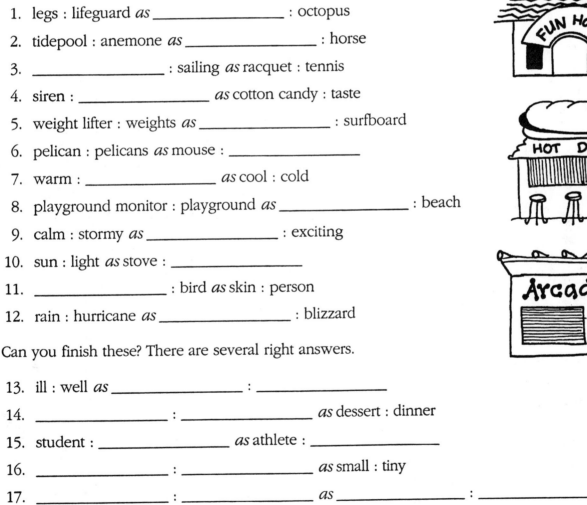

13. ill : well *as* _____ : _____

14. _____ : _____ *as* dessert : dinner

15. student : _____ *as* athlete : _____

16. _____ : _____ *as* small : tiny

17. _____ : _____ *as* _____ : _____

18. _____ : _____ *as* _____ : _____

Name _____

DIGGING UP WORDS

Josiah was lucky enough to find an old treasure map belonging to Billy Bones. Instead of leading him to old, buried treasure, it led him to some words. Where did these words come from?

Many words in the English language are actually borrowed from other countries and cultures. The dictionary tells the origin (beginning place) of many words. Usually this is found at the end of the definition. The most recent place where the word was used is listed first. The earliest origin is given last. Use your dictionary to find out the earliest place each of these words was used.

1. eureka _____
2. shampoo _____
3. cul-de-sac _____
4. status quo _____
5. fiancée _____
6. hors d'oeuvre _____
7. khaki _____
8. Noel _____
9. resume _____
10. veranda _____
11. missile _____
12. diamond _____
13. sandal _____
14. onion _____
15. mosquito _____
16. kindergarten _____
17. ink _____
18. dynamite _____
19. pajama _____
20. tornado _____

Write the meaning of these words.

21. eureka _____
22. cul-de-sac _____
23. hors d'oeuvre _____
24. veranda _____
25. kindergarten _____

**property of
BILLY BONES**

Name

APPENDIX

CONTENTS

GLOSSARY

abalone — a shell lined with mother-of-pearl

abrupt — sudden

accelerate — speed up

accept — to agree to take something

acrophobia — fear of heights

aggravate — to make someone angry; to irritate

ailurophobia — fear of cats

amateur — someone who does something, but is not a professional

anemometer — instrument that measures wind speed

anemone — an invertebrate marine animal

annual — yearly

anthrophobia — fear of flowers

applaud — clap

aquaphobia — fear of water

arachnaphobia — fear of spiders

archipelago — group of islands

architect — person who designs buildings

aroma — an odor

assurance — to tell someone something will be all right

astonish — amaze

astraphobia — fear of lightning or thunderstorms

astronomy — the study of the stars

attorney — lawyer

bandit — robber

banister — railing

bargain — a discussion where each party "wins" something

barometer — instrument that measures air pressure

barracuda — a somewhat dangerous fish

bathyscaphe — a deep-sea research vessel (submarine-like)

biennial — once every two years

biped — an animal with two legs

borscht — a Russian soup made from beets

brooch — a fancy pin (piece of jewelry)

bungalow — small cottage

buoy — floating marker for ships

buoyant — able to float

caddie — person who carries golf clubs for someone

calamity — disaster

carnivore — meat-eating animal

catamaran — a boat with two parallel hulls

cease — stop

chauffeur — someone who is hired to drive someone else

chide — scold

circumference — the distance around the outside of a circle

claustrophobia — fear of closed or small places

coarse — rough; harsh

conceal — hide

conducive — promoting

connoisseur — someone well-informed about a subject

contemplate — think

contrive — make up; figure out

copyright — a license of ownership on a written work

cordial — friendly

coupe — a closed, two-door car

cynophobia — fear of dogs

diagnosis — a description of something that is wrong

diameter — the distance across a circle

dismal — dull, depressing

dreary — dull

eclipse — a partial or full covering of the sun or moon

ecology — the study of natural environments

essential — necessary

euphonium — a tuba-like instrument

except — instead of

famished — very hungry

feat — deed

fjord — a long, narrow inlet of the sea between tall, rocky cliffs

flotsam — floating wreckage from a ship

flounder — kind of fish

foe — enemy

foible — small error or flaw

gam — a school of whales

garish — outlandish; gaudy; tacky

garnish — a decoration, usually something added to a plate of food to make it look attractive

genuine — real

gesture — a movement, usually of the hand

glum — sad, gloomy

gritty — sandy

grotto — cave

habitat — the natural home of a plant or animal

horde — a mob

hurricane — a storm with high winds that begins over water

ichthyologist — a scientist who studies fish

incredible — unbelievable

insurance — something that guarantees help

jeer — laugh at; make fun of

jetsam — rubbish thrown overboard from ships

kelp — a kind of seaweed

kindling — something used to start a fire

lethargic — lazy; sleepy

lexicon — a book of words; dictionary

luminous — shiny

lunar — having to do with the moon

maelstrom — a whirlpool

majority — more than half

manatee — a whale-like animal

manta — a variety of ocean ray

marimba — a xylophone

mariner — a person who works at sea; a sailor

martinet — puppet

massive — huge

matinee — the daytime performance of a play, show, or movie

maw — the wide mouth of a meat-eating animal

merriment — celebration

meteor — rocky burning substance streaking through space

meteorite — a meteor that reaches the Earth's surface

microphobia — fear of germs

minority — less than half

minuscule — tiny

molar — large, back tooth

mollusk — soft-bodied invertebrate, usually protected by a shell

monotonous — tiresome; boring; repetitious

morose — gloomy

murky — dark

mysophobia — fear of dirt

novice — someone who is new at something

numberphobia — fear of numbers

nuptials — wedding

nyctophobia — fear of the dark

obstinate — stubborn

octopod — something with eight feet or limbs

octopus — sea animal with eight tentacles

ophidiophobia — fear of snakes

pacify — to soothe or calm down

patella — kneecap

patent — a license for an invention or product

penalize — to punish

pentapod — something with five feet or limbs

perennials — plants that stay alive or come back each year

perilous — dangerous

phobophobia — fear of fear

plankton — tiny seaweed (or sometimes animals) floating in a body of water

prevaricate — to lie

principal — head of a school

principle — an important or main idea

procession — a moving line-up

prognosis — a guess about what will happen in the future

punctual — on time

pyrophobia — fear of fire

query — a question

revive — to renew or refresh

rubbish — garbage

rumba — a kind of dance

savory — tasty

scoundrel — a person of bad reputation

sequoia — a species of a very large evergreen tree

sieve — a utensil with tiny holes

simmer — to cook at a low heat

snorkel — tube swimmers use for breathing while face is under water

sophomore — someone in the second year of high school or college

soufflé — a light, fluffy food dish made with whipped egg whites

squid — sea animal with ten tentacles around its mouth

stationary — not moving

sternum — breastbone

stethoscope — instrument doctors use to listen to the heart and lungs

stingray — a sea animal with a long, whiplike tail

subpoena — a piece of paper telling someone to come to court

sullen — grumpy

superb — exceptional; excellent

tornado — a funnel-shaped storm that travels across land

tortuous — twisting, winding

translucent — something that light can pass through, but you can't see through it

transparent — something you can see through

treacherous — dangerous

tremulous — fearful

triumph — victory

trophy — a prize

trough — the lowest point of a wave

tsunami — a tidal wave caused by an earthquake

turbid — stirred up and muddy

uncouth — rude, crude

valiant — brave

variable — changeable

vessel — ship or other floating vehicle

vicar — priest in the Church of England

villain — an evil person

volatile — explosive

zoophobia — fear of animals

MEANINGS OF WORD PARTS

PREFIXES

anti ..... (against)	mid ..... (middle)
bene ..... (good)	mini ..... (small)
bi ..... (two)	mis ..... (bad, wrong)
bio ..... (life)	non ..... (without, not)
cent ..... (hundred)	oct ..... (eight)
co ..... (together)	pent ..... (five)
con ..... (with)	post ..... (after)
de ..... (from, away)	pre ..... (before)
dis ..... (wrong, bad)	quart ..... (four)
ex ..... (out)	re ..... (again)
hex ..... (six)	semi ..... (half, part)
il ..... (not)	sub ..... (under, below)
im ..... (not)	super ..... (above)
in ..... (in, into, not)	trans ..... (across)
ir ..... (not)	tri ..... (three)
mal ..... (wrong, bad)	un ..... (not)
micro ..... (small)	uni ..... (one)

SUFFIXES

able, ible ..... (able to be)
ar, er, or, ist ..... (one who)
ary ..... (belonging to)
en ..... (to be made of, to make)
ful ..... (full of, like)
hood, ship ..... (state or quality of)
ion, tion ..... (state of being, act of)
ism, ation ..... (act or quality of)
ize, fy ..... (to cause to be)
less ..... (without)
ly, y ..... (full of, when, how, like)
ment ..... (result, act, or quality of)
ness ..... (state or condition of)
ous, ic, ive ..... (full of, like, pertaining to)
some, like ..... (resembling)
ward ..... (toward)

ROOTS

acro ..... high (acrobat)	geo ..... earth (geology)	photo ..... light (photograph)
act ..... act or do (action)	grad ..... move forward (graduate)	pop ..... people (population)
alti ..... high (altitude)	graph ..... write (autograph)	port ..... carry (portable)
ann ..... year (annual)	grat ..... pleasing (grateful)	posit ..... sit or stay (position)
aqua ..... water (aquaduct)	grav ..... heavy (gravity)	rot ..... turn (rotate)
ast ..... star (astronomy)	jour ..... day (journal)	rupt ..... break (interrupt)
auto ..... self (automatic)	labor ..... work (laboratory)	scend ..... climb (descend)
bene ..... good or well (benefit)	lib ..... book (library)	scrib ..... write (scribble)
bio ..... life (biology)	loc ..... place (location)	scrip ..... write (transcript)
cap ..... head (capital)	lum ..... light (luminous)	sect ..... cut (section)
carn ..... flesh (carnivore)	lun ..... moon (lunar)	sol ..... sun (solar)
civ ..... city (civilization)	mar ..... sea (marine)	son ..... sound (sonic)
cred ..... believe (credible)	meter ..... measure (centimeter)	stat ..... stand (stationary)
cycl ..... circle (bicycle)	mini ..... small (miniscule)	tang ..... touch or feel (tangible)
derm ..... skin (dermatologist)	mob ..... move (mobile)	tard ..... slow (tardy)
dia ..... day (diary)	mon ..... warn (admonish)	tele ..... far (telephone)
dic ..... speak (dictate)	mot ..... move (motion)	temp ..... time (temporary)
dom ..... rule (dominant)	mut ..... change (mutate)	term ..... end (terminate)
don ..... give (donate)	nat ..... born (natural)	therm ..... heat (thermometer)
dorm ..... sleep (dormitory)	nau ..... ship (nautical)	turb ..... spin (turbulent)
dur ..... hard (durable)	nom ..... name (nominate)	vac ..... empty (vacant)
dynam ..... power (dynamite)	oper ..... work (operate)	ver ..... true (verify)
fer ..... bring or carry (transfer)	pac ..... peace (pacify)	verb ..... word (verbal)
fin ..... end (finish)	ped ..... foot (pedal)	vic ..... conquer (victory)
flam ..... fire or burn (flammable)	pend ..... hang (suspend)	vid ..... see (video)
frac ..... break (fracture)	phobia ..... fear (arachnaphobia)	vis ..... see (visual)
frag ..... break (fragment)	phon ..... sound (phonic)	vit ..... life (vital)
fug ..... flee (fugitive)		

Basic Skills/Words & Vocabulary 4-5

WORDS & VOCABULARY
SKILLS TEST

Answer the questions. Each question is worth 1 point.

Write the letter of the word on the right that matches each definition.

_____	1. whirlpool	a. annual
_____	2. odor	b. minuscule
		c. chide
_____	3. to lie	d. microphobia
_____	4. friendly	e. morose
		f. scoundrel
_____	5. on time	g. prevaricate
_____	6. scold	h. famished
		i. shriek
_____	7. very hungry	j. maelstrom
_____	8. dictionary	k. aroma
		l. foe
_____	9. puppet	m. martinet
_____	10. enemy	n. cordial
		o. lexicon
_____	11. fear of germs	p. punctual
		q. claustrophobia
_____	12. gloomy	r. aggravate

Circle the best answer.

13. Which of these would you eat?

      vessel   jetsam   foible   borscht

14. Which would you be likely to find in a church?

      a vicar   a gam   a subpoena   a barracuda

15. Which would you find in the ocean?

      sequoia   flotsam   eclipse   bungalow

16. Which would you choose to help you sail a ship?

      a mariner   a novice   a manatee   a euphonium

17. Would you **aggravate** a villain?   yes   no

18. Which word means **tasty**?

      lunar   tortuous   morose   savory

Name

Circle the word that best fits the blank in each sentence.

19. Amy's _____ remarks hurt everyone's feelings.
        courteous   crude   careful   creative

20. Jake was _____ when he saw how close the shark was to his surfboard.
        horrific   satisfied   terrified   horrible

21. I was surprised by the _____ of a lifeguard on this crowded beach.
        presence   hairdo   tan   absence

22. We laughed when the crab _____ Josie's sunglasses.
        disappeared   snatched   returned   crawled

Tell what you think the words in bold mean as they are used in these sentences.

23. I had never seen a bathing suit quite like the **peculiar** one she wore yesterday.

    I think this word means _____.

24. The **ambidextrous** girl wrote one letter with her left hand and one with her right hand.

    I think this word means _____.

Write the letter of the word on the right that matches each definition.

_____ 25. to make friends	a. hoping	l. phobophobia
_____ 26. a creature with five feet	b. hopeless	m. aquaphobia
_____ 27. to read wrong	c. reread	n. frightful
_____ 28. full of fear	d. misread	o. frighten
_____ 29. one who sails	e. dangerous	p. sharpness
_____ 30. to cause terror	f. friendly	q. sharply
_____ 31. state of being sharp	g. befriend	r. sharper
_____ 32. to make afraid	h. pentapod	s. terrify
_____ 33. fear of water	i. octopod	t. sailor
_____ 34. without hope	j. fearless	u. terrible
_____ 35. full of danger	k. fearful	v. hopeful

Write the letter of the word that has a root that means . . .

_____ 36. flee	a. dynamic	f. fugitive
_____ 37. burn	b. flammable	g. visible
_____ 38. carry	c. transport	h. telegram
_____ 39. act or do	d. descend	i. defend
_____ 40. climb	e. action	j. minivan
_____ 41. see		

Name _____

    57

Write the letter of a synonym for each word below.

_____ 42. novice

_____ 43. cease

_____ 44. foible

_____ 45. valiant

_____ 46. conceal

_____ 47. stationary

_____ 48. tremulous

_____ 49. chide

_____ 50. obstinate

a. scold   g. fearful

b. stop   h. shriek

c. victory   i. immovable

d. stubborn   j. brave

e. flaw   k. hide

f. tremendous   l. beginner

Write the letter of an antonym for each word below.

_____ 51. temporary   a. permanent

_____ 52. sturdy   b. flimsy

_____ 53. careless   c. rude

_____ 54. accelerated   d. speedy

_____ 55. cordial   e. friendly

f. heavy

g. cautious

h. agony

i. slowed

Choose the correct homophone to complete each sentence.

56. Who would like to be _____ (buried, berried) in the sand?

57. I _____ (heard, herd) about your surfing accident.

58. Let's clean up the junk that people _____ (through, threw) on the beach today.

59. My boat's motor died, so my friends _____ (toad, towed) it back to shore.

60. Oh, no! She's headed _____ (strait, straight) for the shark!

Use each of these words to make two compound words.

61. down   _____   _____

62. out   _____   _____

63. light   _____   _____

64. fish   _____   _____

Name

Answer the following questions about denotations and connotations.

65. Circle the connotation of the word **pirate.**
    a. one who robs ships at sea
    b. a mean, ruthless man with a patched eye and a wooden leg who makes people walk the plank

66. Circle the denotation of the word **surf.**
    a. the foamy, breaking waves that are such fun for swimming and jumping
    b. the swelling of the sea that breaks on the shore

67. Read the denotation and connotation. Tell what the word is. _____
    Denotation: the breaking up of a sea-going vessel
    Connotation: crashing into rocks on a wild sea and splitting apart

68. Read the denotation and connotation. Tell what the word is. _____
    Denotation: irritation or blistering caused by exposure to the sun
    Connotation: miserable, painful, red skin that you can't stand to touch

Circle the word that correctly completes each sentence.

69. When they heard about the hurricane coming, Jerod's family decided to buy flood (insurance, assurance).

70. When the ship reached port, the captain dropped the (buoy, anchor).

71. The lifeguard station used a (barometer, anemometer) to measure the speed of the wind at the beach.

72. I've played in the (annual, biennial) beach volleyball tournament every year for the past ten years.

73. Hurry! Run! A (meteor, meteorite) has just hit the beach!

74. I can see through this (translucent, transparent) piece of sea glass.

75. Juna was offered a job as a lifeguard, but she decided not to (except, accept) it.

Choose three of these words. Write two meanings for each word you choose.

fly   trunk   pen   quarter   date   fence   run   light   down   saw   spot   box   fire

word   *meaning 1*   *meaning 2*

76. _____ _____ _____

77. _____ _____ _____

78. _____ _____ _____

Name _____

Write the letter of the figurative language expression that matches each meaning below.

_____ 79. calm down

_____ 80. make you mad

_____ 81. give away a secret

_____ 82. take a chance

_____ 83. start too soon

_____ 84. say something embarrassing

_____ 85. fool around

_____ 86. an argument to have

_____ 87. a bad deal, full of problems

_____ 88. is very expensive

a. spill the beans
b. go bananas
c. cost an arm and a leg
d. red-letter day
e. the last straw
f. a bone to pick
g. drive you up a wall
h. go out on a limb
i. scream bloody murder
j. put a lid on it
k. put your foot in your mouth
l. ham it up
m. jump the gun
n. a real lemon

Cross out the word that does not belong.

89.	anemone	barracuda	lobster	crocodile	squid
90.	sunshine	flashlight	boardwalk	butterfly	camera
91.	mice	artichoke	rainbows	keys	babies

Below is a description of the history and origin of three words. Write the word that matches each one. Choose from the words below.

frankfurter   omelette   comet   sardine   lasagna
spaghetti   cologne   cabbage   tortilla   leotard

_____ 92. from a Greek word meaning "long-haired star"

_____ 93. a Latin word meaning "head"

_____ 94. an Italian word meaning "string"

Finish these analogies.

95. legs : crab *as* _____ : octopus

96. motorcycle : motorcycles *as* _____ : geese

97. melt : _____ *as* compliment : criticize

98. _____ : blizzard *as* rain : monsoon

99. argue : _____ *as* excite : excitement

100. calculator : mathematician *as* surfboard : _____

SCORE: Total Points _____ out of a possible 100 points

Name

WORDS & VOCABULARY
ANSWER KEY

SKILLS TEST

1. j
2. k
3. g
4. n
5. p
6. c
7. h
8. o
9. m
10. l
11. d
12. e
13. borscht
14. a vicar
15. flotsam
16. a mariner
17. no
18. savory
19. crude
20. terrified
21. absence
22. snatched
23–24. Answers will vary.
25. g
26. h
27. d
28. k
29. t
30. s
31. p
32. o
33. m
34. b
35. e
36. f
37. b
38. c
39. e
40. d
41. g
42. l
43. b
44. e
45. j
46. k
47. i
48. g
49. a
50. d
51. a
52. b
53. g
54. i
55. c
56. buried
57. heard
58. threw
59. towed
60. straight
61–64. Answers will vary. See that student makes real words.
65. b
66. b
67. shipwreck
68. sunburn
69. insurance
70. anchor
71. anemometer
72. annual
73. meteorite
74. transparent
75. accept
76–78. Answers will vary. See that student writes 2 correct meanings for each word chosen.
79. j
80. g (or b)
81. a
82. h
83. m
84. k
85. l
86. f
87. n
88. c
89. crocodile (others are sea animals)
90. camera (others are compound words)
91. artichoke (others are plurals)
92. comet
93. cabbage
94. spaghetti
95. tentacles
96. goose
97. freeze
98. snow
99. argument
100. surfer

SKILLS EXERCISES

page 10

Answers may vary some, depending on student's opinions.

1. yes
2. no
3. no
4. no
5. no
6. no
7. yes
8. no
9. no
10. yes
11. yes
12. no
13. no
14. no
15. no

page 11

Answers may vary some, depending on student's opinions.

1. no
2. yes
3. no
4. no
5. yes
6. no
7. yes
8. Answers will vary.
9. Answers will vary.
10. yes
11. yes
12. throw out
13. no
14. Answers will vary.
15. no

page 12

1. b
2. c
3. b
4. b
5. b
6. c
7. b
8. a
9. a
10. a
11. c
12. a
13. b

page 13

1. a
2. b
3. a
4. c
5. c
6. a
7. b
8. a
9. b
10. a
11. b
12. b
13. a

page 14

1. fry it for lunch
2. feed it to a fish
3. take it swimming
4. put it in a jewelry box
5. avoid it
6. explore it
7. find an answer to it
8. dance it
9. bake it
10. show it off
11. slide on it
12. make music on it
13. make friends with it
14. send it to school
15. pour water through it
16. hire it

page 15

A aquaphobia
M nyctophobia
N acrophobia
H pyrophobia
J ophidiophobia
I numberphobia
L anthrophobia
C ailurophobia
F arachnaphobia
B cynophobia
O claustrophobia
D astraphobia
E microphobia
K mysophobia
G zoophobia

page 16

Down
1. abalone
2. ecology
3. habitat
4. grotto
7. tsunami
8. mariner
10. weed

Across
5. trough
6. ichthyologist
9. flotsam
11. archipelago
12. fjord
13. sea

page 17

Answers may vary. Check to see that student's definitions are similar and that items are correctly colored in the picture.

vessel—a ship or other floating vehicle—boat—blue
lunar—having to do with the moon—moon—yellow
luminous—shiny—moon, stars, or fire—orange
biped—an animal with two legs—any of the persons—red
savory—tasty—marshmallows—white
merriment—celebration—any of the dancers—green
pentapod—something with five feet or limbs—starfish—pink
gritty—sandy—sand—beige
murky—dark—water—gray
kindling—something used to start a fire—wood—brown

page 18

Answers will vary on the guesses. Definitions may vary somewhat also. Definitions should be similar to these:
1. to renew or refresh
2. stirred up and muddy
3. changeable
4. twisting, winding
5. not moving
6. gloomy
7. explosive
8. unbelievable
9. rude or crude
10. tiny

page 19

Answers may vary somewhat.

1. intended
2. washed; huge
3. bridge
4. tornado
5. tossed; storm
6. dragged; hid
7. ocean; earthquake
8. tail; ship
9. crashed; sank
10. mystery

page 20

1. one wheel or one cycle
2. on shore
3. make friends
4. below normal
5. spell wrong
6. too high (or too much) price
7. middle of the field
8. against war
9. across the Atlantic
10. on foot
11. write again
12. before dawn
13. many colors
14. not possible
15. small van
16. between states
17. not friendly
18. not honest

page 21

Check to see that student has drawn the correct items.

page 22

excitement—act of being excited or exciting
perilous—full of peril
rocky—full of rocks
stormy—like a storm
frighten—to make afraid
nervous—full of nerves
horrific—pertaining to horror
seaward—toward the sea
hardship—state of being hard
fearful—full of fear
courageous—full of courage
survivor—one who survives
hopeless—without hope
dangerous—full of danger
sailor—one who sails
droplets—small drops
terrify—to cause terror
lostness—state of being lost
troublesome—full of trouble
heroism—act of being a hero

page 23

1. treacherous
2. diver
3. magical
4. deepen
5. frighten
Answer: A tiger shark.
6. skyward
7. hungry
8. oceanic
9. breakable
10. sharpness
Answer: A whale shark.

page 24

1. carn
2. phobia
3. fug
4. mon
5. vis
6. aqua
7. act
8. flam
9. scend
10. dynam
11. dorm
12. tele
13. port
14. labor
15. phobia
16. port
17. phobia
18. scend

page 25

Answers will vary. Check to see that student has formed real words.

page 26

Path should follow these word pairs:
rubbish—garbage
infant—newborn
bandit—robber
applaud—clap
dull—dreary
precise—exact
triumph—victory
essential—necessary

page 27

1. exciting
2. novice
3. deed
4. unbelievable
5. peril
6. amaze
7. huge
8. answer
9. drool
10. real
11. movement
12. mob
13. terror
14. diary
15. punish

page 28

1. destroy
2. meek
3. receive
4. cheerful
5. calm
6. defend
7. divide
8. mischief
9. express
10. timid
11. tender
12. proceed

page 29

Correct pairs are:
sleeping—slumbering
snooze—doze
restful—tranquil
soothe—pacify
scorch—blister
speedy—hasty
agony—torment
sudden—abrupt
cautious—careful
heal—mend
think—contemplate
pain—hurt
flat—level
hide—conceal
Sentences will vary.

page 30

Answers will vary slightly.
1. best
2. good
3. expensive
4. Aunt
5. crooked
6. buy; beautiful; new
7. heavy
8. permanent
9. generous
10. sturdy
11. unusual
12. strong

page 31

Answers will vary, depending on which word student chooses to change. Most likely possibilities are:
Tom's Nightmare
Eat at Bob's Diner—Great (or good, or wonderful) Food
S.S. Sunset
Danger, Deep Water!
Please Do Not Throw Trash On The Beach
No Sleeping On The Beach
Beach Open 9 A.M. – 9 P.M.

Mystery at Crooked River
The Biggest Dragon
Burglar Steals Jewelry
Earthquake Hits at Noon

page 32

Top answer: The Hole in the Pail
1. bury
2. straight
3. threw
4. caught
5. seas
6. foul
7. pail; break
8. pier; hour
9. beat
10. taught
11. buy; some
12. cents
13. feet
14. flew
15. flee

page 33

Top answer: a wail
1. see; sea
2. son; sun
3. heard; herd
4. steal; steel
5. Would; wood
6. groan; grown
7. weak; week
8. not; knot
9. ate; eight
10. close; clothes
11. toe; tow
12. sore; soar

page 34

Answers will vary. Check to see that student has used homophones accurately.

page 35

Answers will vary. Check to see that student has formed real compound words.

page 36

Definitions may vary slightly.
1. small sea creature; to grouch
2. down
3. track
4. a fruit; an outing with another person; a particular day
5. spring
6. fire
7. a flying insect; to soar up in the air
8. spot
9. rain; a place to wash
10. pen
11. container; sport where people hit each other with gloves
12. tick

page 37

Top answers:
1–2. a lead or important person; shape with 5 points
Other answers will vary. Check to see that student has accurately illustrated 2 or more meanings of the three words chosen.

page 38

1. squid
2. dessert
3. buoy
4. astronomy
5. antonyms
6. biennial
7. insurance
8. anemometer
9. flotsam
10. complaint
11. meteorite

page 39

1. minority
2. diagnosis
3. simmer
4. annuals
5. principal
6. copyright
7. circumference
8. hurricane
9. translucent
10. accept

page 40

Answers will vary somewhat. See that student has the general idea of the meaning of each figurative language expression.
It's raining cats and dogs.—It's raining hard.
You drive me up a wall.—You're really bothering me.
Go out on a limb.—Take a chance.
I have a bone to pick with you.—I'm mad at you about something.
You've spilled the beans.—You've told something you should not have.
Don't jump the gun.—Don't be in such a hurry.
She's lost her head!—She's acting out of control.
My car's a real lemon!—My car has lots of problems; it was a bad deal.

page 41

Answers will vary somewhat. See that student has the general idea of the meaning of each figurative language expression.
Jay likes to ham it up.—Jay likes to act wild and crazy.
What a backseat driver!—Someone else in the car tells the driver how to drive.
She's got her nose in a book.—She's reading and ignoring everything else.
Don't lose your cool.—Don't lose your temper.
This will cook your goose!—This will really make you mad.
It's the last straw!—It's the last of many things to go wrong.
Keep a lid on it!—Keep from getting mad or being too noisy or wild.
You've put your foot in your mouth again.—You've said something stupid or embarrassing.

page 42

There are 24 examples of figurative language.
cost me an arm and a leg;
sun beating on me;
pounding like drums;
squawking as loud as a choir;
chip off the old block;
pretty as a picture;
faster than greased lightning;
dry as dust;
dull as a doorknob;
red-letter day;
go bananas;
blow her top;
off her rocker;
take the cake;
breaking up ships like toothpicks;
scared stiff;
screaming bloody murder;
last straw;
Out of sight, out of mind;
absence makes the heart grow fonder;
quick as a wink;
make no bones about it;
wipeout;
deader than a doornail

page 43

"Fragile" is the word that does not fit. Description of classification categories may vary.
1. lizard; mammals or animals in the sea
2. chowder; things floating in the ocean
3. bandit; things on a boat
4. wind; kinds of precipitation
5. lobster; kinds of birds
6. mumble; loud noises or screams
7. ruler; computer parts
8. wrench; kitchen utensils or equipment
9. scorpion; sea animals
10. cactus; things you see on a beach
11. receiver; parts of a book
12. spaghetti; parts of the body
13. redwood; kinds of fish
14. attorney; church leaders
15. stumble; words that mean jump
16. duck; baby animals
17. hazard; kinds of storms
18. frog; reptiles

page 44

Answers will vary, particularly the connotations. Denotations are listed here:
Pirate—someone who robs ships
Sunburn—irritation or blistering of the skin from the sun
Shark—a kind of dangerous fish
Storm—bad weather accompanied by wind and some precipitation such as rain or snow
Island—land surrounded on all sides by water

page 45

1. ocean, D,C
2. iceberg, C,D
3. swim, C,D
4. octopus, D,C
5. lifeboat, D,C
6. vacation, C,D
7. money, D,C

page 46

Answers will vary depending upon what information student can find about the words.

1. named after G. W. G. Ferris, an American engineer
2. named after William Frisbee, a pie company owner
3. named after Mars, the Roman god of war
4. means "day of the moon"
5. Greek word meaning "messenger"
6. named after R. J. L. Guppy, a man who loved animals
7. named after the city of Cologne, which makes perfume; means "water of Cologne"
8. named after French botanist Pierre Magnol
9. named after President Theodore (Teddy) Roosevelt, who rescued a bear cub
10. from a French word that means "crane's foot"
11. named after a French acrobat, Jules Léotard, who wore tights for his acts
12. from a Greek word meaning "long-haired star"
13. from a Greek word for a plant that people used as a writing surface
14. named after Sardinia, an island off Italy
15. named after a state in Mexico
16. named after the explorer Amerigo Vespucci

page 47

Answers will vary depending upon what information students are able to find.

1. Greek word meaning "made from barley"
2. named after a vegetarian named Sylvester Graham; means "made from wheat flour"
3. named after Frankfurt, Germany, where they were first made
4. Latin meaning "round swelling"
5. German word meaning "wafer" (Supposedly first "invented" when a knight in armor sat on a pancake.)
6. Portuguese and Spanish word for a plant in Guinea
7. French word meaning "thin blade of a sword," because the omelettes were thin
8. Spanish word meaning "round cake"
9. named after city of Tangiers
10. French word meaning "moss"
11. Latin word meaning "head," because cabbage is shaped like a head
12. Aztec word meaning "bitter water"
13. Italian word meaning "string"
14. Portuguese and Spanish word meaning "residue or leftover substance"

page 48

Answers may vary somewhat.

1. feet
2. sunscreen
3. pocket
4. breathe
5. eat
6. lake, pool, or ocean
7. cupboard, cabinet, or china cabinet
8. break
9. trees
10. temperature
11. water
12. book
13. feet, paws, or legs
14. broom

page 49

Answers may vary somewhat.

1. tentacles
2. pasture, barn, or field
3. sail or sailboat
4. hear
5. surfer
6. mice
7. hot
8. lifeguard
9. dull
10. heat
11. feathers
12. snow
13–18. Answers will vary. Check to see that the pairs form accurate analogies.

page 50

Answers may vary depending upon what resources student has available.

1. Greek
2. Hindu or Indian
3. French
4. Latin
5. French
6. French
7. Persian
8. Latin
9. Latin
10. Latin
11. Latin
12. Greek
13. Persian
14. Latin
15. Spanish or Latin
16. German
17. German
18. Greek
19. Indian, Hindu, or Persian
20. Spanish
21–25. Answers will vary somewhat.
21. "I found it!"
22. a dead-end street
23. appetizer
24. porch with a roof
25. school for young children